Jesus
God's Son, Savior, Lord

EUGENE CHAMBERLAIN • ILLUSTRATED BY **JAMES PADGETT**

BROADMAN PRESS
Nashville, Tennessee

Dewey Decimal Classification: J 232.9
Subject heading: JESUS CHRIST — BIOGRAPHY
Printed in the United States of America

Contents

When Jesus Was a Child

"Mary," the angel Gabriel spoke. The young woman's eyes grew large with wonder.

"You are chosen to be the mother of God's own Son. You must call his name Jesus, for he shall save his people from their sin."

Many Jewish girls hoped to become the mother of God's Promised One. Long centuries before Mary lived, God's prophets told about his coming. Now God's promises were about to be kept.

But Mary was puzzled. "How can I become a mother?" she asked. "I don't have a husband."

Then Gabriel answered. "This child will be a special child. His father is to be God himself."

Mary was engaged to marry a man named Joseph. When Joseph found out that Mary was expecting a baby, he was upset. An angel explained to him who Mary's child would be. Joseph began at once to plan how to take care of Mary and the baby.

At this time the Roman government required every Jewish man to go to the city where his ancestors had lived. There the men were to be enrolled for taxes. Joseph and Mary decided that she would make the long trip to Bethlehem with him.

By the time they arrived in Bethlehem, the baby was almost ready to be born. Joseph could not find a place to stay, so he took Mary to a freshly cleaned stable. Jesus was born there that very night.

On a hillside just east of Bethlehem, shepherds were tending their sheep. Suddenly an angel appeared to them.

"Don't be afraid," the angel said. "I have come to give you the great good news that the Savior is born. He is Jesus, the Christ. And you can find him in a stable in Bethlehem." When the angel finished speaking, other angels joined him. "Glory to God in the highest; peace be to men of good will," they sang.

As soon as the angels left, the shepherds hurried to Bethlehem. There they found the baby just as the angel had said.

Months later important visitors came to worship Jesus. They had followed a special star that signaled the birth of a new king. When the star stood still above the house where Jesus was, they went in and worshiped the child. They gave him three gifts: gold, frankincense, and myrrh. Then they left for their homeland.

That very night an angel warned Joseph that King Herod would try to kill the baby. Joseph quickly took Mary and Jesus to Egypt, where Herod could not harm Jesus.

After King Herod died, Joseph took Mary and Jesus to Nazareth. There Jesus grew up.

When Jesus was twelve years old, he went with his parents to Jerusalem for the Feast of the Passover. After the celebration, Joseph and Mary started home with many other people from their part of the country. Each of them thought Jesus was walking with the other. When night came, they missed him. Returning to Jerusalem, they found Jesus in the Temple. He was talking to the teachers there. Jesus explained that he was doing the work of his Father, God. After that Jesus returned to Nazareth with Mary and Joseph to finish growing up.

Thinkback: If you knew about Jesus only what you have read so far, what would you know? Complete these blanks to be sure.

Jesus is the _____ of _____.

The birth of Jesus is good news for _____ of earth's _____.

Jesus came to _____ people from sin.

Starting His Special Work

When Jesus was thirty years old, he knew the time had come for him to do the special work God wanted him to do. The first thing Jesus did at this time was to go to the Jordan River, where his cousin John the Baptist was preaching. "I have come to be baptized by you," Jesus told John. As Jesus came up out of the water, God spoke. "This is my beloved Son. Listen to him." Also the Holy Spirit in the form of a dove landed on Jesus' head.

After his baptism, Jesus went all by himself to a wild and lonely spot. For forty days he went without food as he prayed. At the end of forty days, the devil came to try to get Jesus to give up his plan to give his life to save men from sin. Each time the devil made a suggestion, Jesus answered by quoting words from the Old Testament. Finally the devil left Jesus alone for a time.

Soon afterwards Jesus attended a wedding in Cana. There he performed his first miracle. When the wine was gone, Jesus changed some water to wine. The wedding party could then continue.

When time for the Passover came, Jesus went to Jerusalem. One night Nicodemus, an important Jewish leader, came to see him. Jesus explained to Nicodemus how to be saved. "God so loves the world," Jesus said, "that he has given his only Son so that all men who trust their lives to the Son will have eternal life."

On the way back to Galilee, Jesus went through Samaria. By Jacob's well at Sychar Jesus talked with a sinful woman. She realized that he was the Son of God and ran to bring other villagers to see him.

Jesus went again to Cana. An officer of the king came to Jesus. "Come to Capernaum, please, and heal my son," he begged.

"Go on home," Jesus told him, "your son will live."

A bit later Jesus visited Nazareth, the town where he had grown up. On the sabbath he went to the synagogue. The ruler of the synagogue invited him to read the Scriptures and to speak. Jesus read from the book of Isaiah. He read verses that described God's Promised One. Jesus told the people that the words described him and his work.

The people became angry. They thought of Jesus as the son of Joseph, the carpenter. They could not believe that he was anyone special.

After this Jesus made Capernaum his headquarters. There he healed a man possessed by demons, Peter's mother-in-law, and many others. Then he toured all of Galilee in the company of Peter, Andrew, James, and John.

Jesus decided to select some of his followers or disciples to receive special training. After he prayed all night, he chose Simon Peter, Andrew, James and John, Philip, Bartholomew, Matthew, Thomas, James the son of Alphaeus, Simon Zelotes, Judas the son of James, and Judas Iscariot. These were the twelve apostles.

One day a large number of people gathered around Jesus at a level spot on a mountain. There he explained what it means to be his follower. "Treat others as you want them to treat you. Put doing God's will first in your life. Trust God to care for you day by day," he said. "Live a perfect life because God himself is perfect."

One day in Capernaum a Roman centurion asked Jesus to heal his servant. Jesus offered to go to the centurion's home. But the man said, "You don't need to do that. Say the word and my servant will be healed." Jesus did exactly that.

Soon afterwards Jesus visited Nain. As he came near the town, a funeral procession came along the road. The only son of a widow was dead. "Don't cry," Jesus said to the man's mother. Then standing beside the body, he said, "Young man, get up."

The young man sat up and began talking to the people around him.

Thinkback: Review this section of your book. Can you find examples of these things which Jesus came to do:

Preach good news to the poor

Tell people how to be free of sin

Give sight to the blind

Show people how to live happy lives

If you do not find examples of each term in this section, keep looking as you read other sections.

Teaching and Helping People

Jesus told the people many stories about everyday things. Each story, or parable, helped them understand some truth about God.

One time at the end of a hard day of teaching, Jesus suggested that he and his twelve apostles sail across the Sea of Galilee. Jesus was so tired that he fell asleep in the boat. A sudden storm swept down on the boat. Wind whipped the sea into mountainous waves. The twelve awoke Jesus. "Don't you care that we are about to die?" they said.

Jesus got up. "Be still," he said to the wind and waves. Immediately the storm ceased.

When Jesus returned to Capernaum, he continued helping people. He raised a twelve-year-old girl who had died. And he healed a woman who had been ill for twelve years.

One day Jesus called the twelve together. "I have a job for you. Go out in teams of two. Do as I do: teach, and preach, and heal the sick." And this is what they did.

Through the next summer Jesus gave special training to the twelve. He prepared them to carry on his work after he returned to heaven.

One day a large throng of people followed them to an out-of-the-way place. Jesus taught the crowd all day long.

"Master, send the people away. They need food," the disciples urged him.

Andrew said, "A boy here has five rolls made from barley and two fish. Can that help?" This was all the food the disciples could find.

Then Jesus had all the people sit down on the grass. He took the rolls and fish. First, he asked God to bless the food. Then he began breaking the food into pieces. There was enough food for all five thousand of the people.

Many people thought Jesus meant to overthrow the Roman government and be an earthly king. They tried to make Jesus do just that. When he refused, these people quit following him.

Jesus wanted the twelve to understand who he truly was. So he asked them this question: "Who do people think I am?"

They gave several answers, But none said that Jesus was the Son of God, the Promised One.

Then Jesus asked, "Who do you think I am?"

"You are the Christ, the son of the living God," Peter answered for the group. They were beginning to understand.

One day Jesus took Peter, James, and John with him high on the slopes of a mountain. The three were amazed to see Jesus' face turn to dazzling white. They were even more amazed when they saw Elijah and Moses talking with Jesus. Peter wanted to build little shacks for Jesus, Moses, and Elijah and just stay there.

Suddenly the voice of God spoke: "This is
my beloved Son; listen to all he says."

27

One day at Capernaum the disciples began fussing among themselves. Each expected to be an important person in Jesus' kingdom. Each was jealous of the others.

"You must be like a little child," Jesus told the disciples. "The person who will be great in my kingdom must spend his time in helping others."

A little later Jesus called together seventy of his followers. He gave them instruction to go out in teams of two to teach and preach and heal. When they returned, each team eagerly gave its report to the others.

One day a messenger came to Jesus from his friends Mary and Martha of Bethany. "Please come," they asked. "Our brother Lazarus is very ill."

In two days Jesus started to Bethany. The disciples were worried about his going near Jerusalem. They knew the religious leaders wanted to stop Jesus from teaching about the kingdom of God. But Jesus was determined to go.

When Jesus and the disciples reached Bethany, they found that Lazarus had died and had been buried. Jesus went to the tomb. Standing at the entrance, he said, "Lazarus, come out."

Lazarus did. The people were all amazed. But the Jewish high court was more determined than ever to get rid of Jesus.

For a time Jesus left that part of the country to escape the high court. Yet all the time Jesus knew that he had to go to Jerusalem to give his message to the people. He decided to go there when Jews came from all over the world to observe the Feast of the Passover.

Jesus and his disciples started on the dusty, steep road from Jericho to Jerusalem. Right at the city gate sat Bartimaeus, a blind beggar. When he knew that Jesus was near, he began to call out for help. The people tried to quiet him, but he kept on yelling.

Jesus stopped. "Bring him here," he said. When the people brought Bartimaeus to him, Jesus asked, "What do you want me to do for you?"

"Give me my sight, Master," Bartimaeus answered.

Jesus replied. "Your faith in me has brought you your sight." And that instant Bartimaeus could see.

Thinkback: What do you think was the most important thing God sent Jesus to do? Write your answer in the margin of this page or on a separate sheet of paper. Remember to check your answer again after you finish reading the entire book.

Dying and Living Again

When Jesus and his friends reached
Bethphage, a little way east of Jerusalem,
Jesus sent two of them to bring a donkey colt
to him. The disciples placed some of their
garments on the colt's back, and Jesus rode
into Jerusalem. Along the way, people spread
palm branches in the road, just as if Jesus were
an earthly king. They yelled, "Hosanna,"
which means "Save us, we pray."

By the time the procession reached the Temple, even the children were singing praises.

During the week which followed, Jesus tried to help his friends understand what was about to happen. Each day he taught large numbers of people in the Temple.

Only the fear of the people stopped the religious leaders from getting rid of Jesus. Instead of harming him physically, they asked him hard questions. They hoped his answers would turn the people against him. But they were never able to trap him this way.

Judas Iscariot, however, was unhappy with Jesus. He decided to help Jesus' enemies find a good time and place to arrest him. The enemies paid Judas thirty pieces of silver for his help.

On Thursday evening Jesus and the disciples went to a quiet room where they were to eat the Passover meal. In those days people wore sandals, and a good host saw that his guests' feet were washed when they came to a party. Just before the meal Jesus washed the feet of each disciple.

Sometime during the meal Judas left. He was ready to tell Jesus' enemies where and how they could arrest Jesus.

35

Jesus took some of the bread from the meal. He broke it into pieces, giving each disciple a piece. "Eat this," he told them. "This is my body." He passed a cup among them. "Drink this," he told them. "It is my blood. I will give both for you. Do these two things in remembrance of me." This was the first Lord's Supper.

Jesus then told the disciples many things about the days ahead. He told them that he loved them. He said he would die for them and for others. He prayed for them and for all who would later become his followers. After a time they left the room and walked to the garden of Gethsemane in brilliant moonlight.

In the quiet garden Jesus took Peter, James, and John with him deep into the shadows of the olive trees. "Stay here," he said to them, "while I go over there and pray." Then he walked slowly to the very heart of the garden. There he prayed, "If there is a way for me to avoid dying, let me live. But what you want, Father, I will do."

After Jesus prayed this way for the third time, he could see torches flickering through the trees. The religious leaders were bringing Roman soldiers to arrest him. At the head of the line was Judas.

"Master," Judas said. Then he gave Jesus a kiss, the way a person often greeted his teacher. The kiss signaled the soldiers which man to arrest. All of the disciples ran away. But Peter followed Jesus at a distance to see what would happen next.

First, Jesus was brought before Annas, the ex-high priest. After Annas asked Jesus a few questions, Jesus was taken before the Jewish high court, the Sanhedrin.

The time was very early on Friday morning. The court could not legally pass the death sentence. But it did decide that Jesus should die.

To make the sentence legal, the court needed the approval of the Roman governor. So Jesus was taken to Pilate. There his enemies accused him of planning to overthrow the Romans. Pilate knew this was not so, but he was afraid of the stories that would be told to the Roman emperor. Pilate finally gave in and sentenced Jesus.

The Roman soldiers led Jesus away. They
put a purple robe on him because kings wore
purple. They placed a crown of thorns on his
head. They gave him a reed to hold as a king
holds a scepter. Then they made fun of him,
spat on him, and hit him on the head.

Then the soldiers forced Jesus to drag his cross through the streets toward the place of execution. At last the procession reached the hill called the Place of the Skull. There they nailed him to his cross.

For six hours Jesus hung on the cross. In spite of awful pain, he asked John to care for his mother, Mary. He prayed for God to forgive the people. "They don't know what they are doing," he said. At last he screamed one final cry of pain. "It is finished," he exclaimed.

The Roman in charge of the execution could only say, "Truly, this was the Son of God."

Joseph of Arimathea placed the body of Jesus in his own tomb in a nearby garden. A big stone was rolled over the entrance to the tomb, the tomb was sealed, and Roman soldiers were placed on guard.

The next Sunday morning, Mary Magdalene and Mary, Jesus' mother, and other women came to the tomb. They wanted to be sure his body was properly buried. When they arrived, the stone was rolled away. Jesus had risen from the dead.

During the next forty days Jesus appeared to his followers in different places. One day Jesus appeared to more than five hundred of his followers on a mountain in Galilee. "Go everywhere, winning other followers for me," he said. "Teach them all the things I have taught you. Baptize them in the name of the Father, and the Son, and the Holy Spirit."

Jesus last appeared on the Mount of Olives. While the disciples watched, he was taken up in a cloud. Suddenly they were aware of the presence of two men in white.

"Why stand gazing into heaven?" the men asked. Remembering Jesus' command to tell all men everywhere about him, they returned to Jerusalem.

Thinkback: Pretend to be one of the disciples. Write how you feel now that you know Jesus is alive forevermore. What will you do now that Jesus has returned to heaven?

ROME

EPHESUS

CORINTH

MALTA

TARSUS

ANTIOCH

DAMAS·

CYPRUS

CAPERN·

·NAZARETH

JERUSALE·

BETHLEHEM·

EGYPT

SOME NEW TESTAMENT PLACES

Reflections

You have read about only some of the things which Jesus said and did. You find more about him in the four Gospels: Matthew, Mark, Luke, and John.

Many people know stories about Jesus. Many people can tell you things which Jesus said. But just knowing these things is not enough. You must also ask yourself this question: What should I do as a result of reading this book?

You may need to talk with your parents, your teachers at church, or your pastor about how to become a Christian.

If you are already a Christian, think about ways you can share the story of Jesus with others. One way is to share this book. Another way is to tell what you know to your brothers and sisters, to other relatives, and to friends.

Read the book again if you need to, in order to understand what you should do.